DRAW, MODEL, & PAINT

MODELING DINOSAURS

by Isidro Sánchez
Models by Roser Piñol
Photographs by Juan Carlos Martínez

Gareth Stevens Publishing
MILWAUKEE

For a free color catalog describing Gareth Stevens' list of high-quality books,
call 1-800-542-2595 (USA) or 1-800-461-9120 (Canada).
Gareth Stevens' Fax: 414-225-0377.

Library of Congress Cataloging-in-Publication Data available upon request from the publisher.
Fax: 414-225-0377 for the attention of the Publishing Records Department.

ISBN 0-8368-1518-1

This North American edition first published in 1996 by
Gareth Stevens Publishing
1555 North RiverCenter Drive, Suite 201
Milwaukee, Wisconsin 53212, USA

Original edition © 1994 Ediciones Este, S.A., Barcelona, Spain, under the title
Modela Dinosaurios. Text by Isidro Sánchez. Models by Roser Piñol.
Photography by Juan Carlos Martínez. All additional material supplied for
this edition © 1996 by Gareth Stevens, Inc.

Series editor: Barbara J. Behm
Editorial assistants: Jamie Daniel, Diane Laska, Rita Reitci

Printed in the United States of America

1 2 3 4 5 6 7 8 9 99 98 97 96

CONTENTS

Media for modeling

WIRE MODELING TOOL

Modeling clay

Modeling clay comes in different-sized blocks. When you purchase modeling clay from an art supply store, make sure to buy the kind that does not need to be baked.

CLAY BLOCKS

Pictured are blocks of modeling clay, a wire modeling tool, and palette knives. The modeling tool has wires on both ends. It is used for hollowing out or scooping clay. Palette knives are used for separating, cutting, and smoothing clay.

PALETTE KNIVES

Plaster of Paris

PLASTER OF PARIS ROLL

Plaster of Paris comes in rolls you can purchase from an art supply store.

Plaster of Paris is a type of modeling plaster that is used to completely cover an object. First, a frame is constructed. Then the frame is covered with Plaster of Paris. The material is designed to be shaped when it is wet.

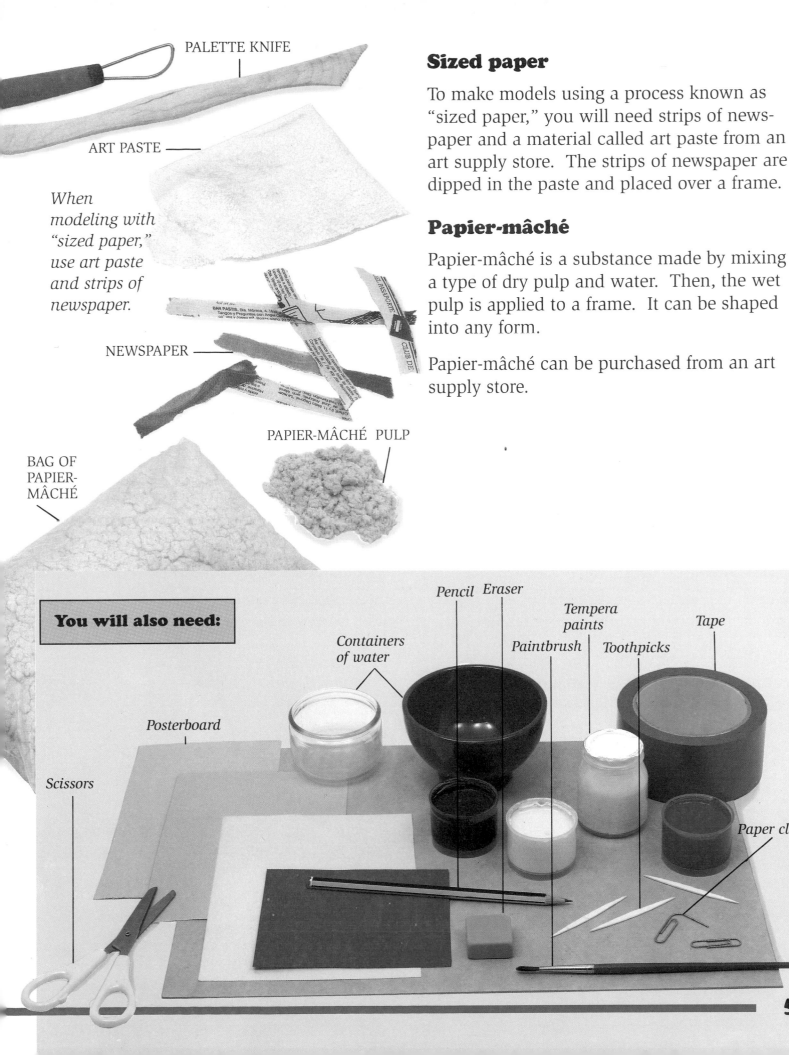

PALETTE KNIFE

ART PASTE

When modeling with "sized paper," use art paste and strips of newspaper.

NEWSPAPER

BAG OF PAPIER-MÂCHÉ

PAPIER-MÂCHÉ PULP

Sized paper

To make models using a process known as "sized paper," you will need strips of newspaper and a material called art paste from an art supply store. The strips of newspaper are dipped in the paste and placed over a frame.

Papier-mâché

Papier-mâché is a substance made by mixing a type of dry pulp and water. Then, the wet pulp is applied to a frame. It can be shaped into any form.

Papier-mâché can be purchased from an art supply store.

You will also need:

Pencil Eraser

Tempera paints

Tape

Containers of water

Paintbrush Toothpicks

Posterboard

Scissors

Paper clips

Modeling dinosaurs

Modeling clay

Modeling clay is a material that can be easily shaped. If the model you are making is large, like some of the dinosaurs in this book, you may need to add support to the clay with toothpicks and paper clips.

MODELING CLAY COMES IN VARIOUS COLORS.

ROLLED MEDIUM

ROLLED THIN

ROLLED THICK

The more you roll out a piece of clay, the longer and thinner it will be.

Make strips of clay by rolling out pieces with the palm of your hand on a table. Pieces of clay can be joined together with slip. Slip is made by mixing small chunks of clay with water until a paste forms. Slip makes a perfect glue for clay. Wait a day for modeling clay to dry before painting.

Sometimes it will be necessary to hollow out a model so that it is not as heavy. This is done with a wire modeling tool, as shown.

WIRE MODELING TOOL

CLAY BLOCK

 SLIP

Plaster of Paris

For the dinosaur models in this book that use Plaster of Paris, cut fairly short strips from the roll, as shown. Then put the strips in water for a few seconds. Next, cover the dinosaur model with the strips. Wait an hour or so for the plaster to dry before painting the model.

ROLL OF PLASTER OF PARIS

STRIP OF PLASTER

Place the plaster strips in water for just a few seconds. If they are in the water too long, they will not stick to the frame.

Sized paper

For the dinosaur models made of sized paper, put a small amount of art paste in a container and add water according to the directions on the package. Cut some short strips of newspaper, and put them in the container for a few seconds until they have absorbed some of the paste. Cover the dinosaur frame with the strips. The strips will stick easily. Wait at least a day for the material to dry before painting.

ADD WATER A LITTLE AT A TIME.

NEWSPAPER STRIPS

To cover the entire surface of a model with sized paper, use short strips and apply the strips carefully.

PAPIER-MÂCHÉ PULP

Papier-mâché

To model dinosaurs with papier-mâché, put some dry pulp in a bowl. Add water a little at a time until the substance is smooth. Then let the pulp sit for about an hour. Next, cover the model with a thin layer of the pulp. When this has dried, apply a second layer. Then, let the model dry for about four days before painting.

An enormous Diplodocus

2. Roll out a smaller piece of clay. Fold it in half. This will become the dinosaur's back legs.

1. Shape a large ball of blue modeling clay, as shown at left. This will become the main part of the dinosaur's body.

You will need:
- modeling clay
- palette knives
- a paper clip

3. Roll out two more pieces for the front legs. Roll out a piece for the tail that is thick at one end and thin at the other.

4. Join the legs and tail to the main body, as shown. Press the pieces firmly together.

5. Smooth over the connections with your fingers and a palette knife.

6. Roll out a long, thick piece of clay for the neck. Join the neck to the body. If you have trouble attaching the neck, use a paper clip for support, as shown.

7. Make bumpy scales on the back of the neck by removing clay with a palette knife, as shown. Then use your fingers to help shape the scales.

8. Smooth the entire dinosaur with a palette knife. Then add texture to the skin, as shown, by making marks in the clay with a palette knife.

9. Add teeth, eyes, and toes made of white and black clay. Finally, decorate the dinosaur by pressing on pieces of clay in different colors.

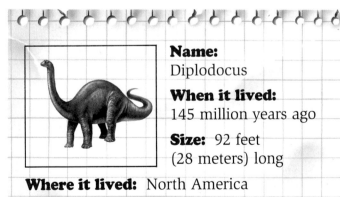

Name: Diplodocus

When it lived: 145 million years ago

Size: 92 feet (28 meters) long

Where it lived: North America

Characteristics: Diplodocus was a huge herbivore. It was not as wide as some dinosaurs, but it was longer than a tennis court. Its long neck allowed it to reach the leaves of tall trees. Fossil remains of Diplodocus can be seen in museums throughout the world.

A hard-headed Pachycephalosaurus

You will need:
- modeling clay
- palette knives
- a small container
- a paintbrush
- tempera paints

2. With a palette knife, cut away any unwanted clay. Then continue to shape the dinosaur with your hands.

1. Mold a piece of clay until it is similar to the shape above.

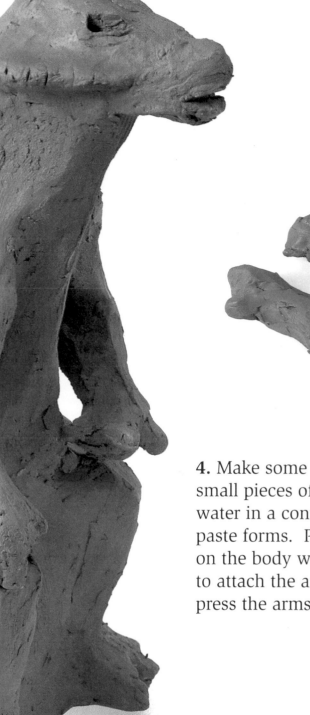

3. Roll out two pieces of clay for the arms. Use a palette knife to shape the claws, as shown.

4. Make some slip by mixing small pieces of clay and water in a container until a paste forms. Put some slip on the body where you want to attach the arms. Then press the arms into the slip.

5. Add details to the head with a palette knife.

7. Shape the claws of the legs with a palette knife.

8. Paint the dinosaur, except for its head, with yellow tempera paint. Add brown stripes to the body, and paint the claws white. Before changing colors, let the previous color dry. Be sure to wash your paintbrush between colors.

6. Form the legs by removing clay from the model.

10. Let the Pachycephalosaurus dry before it butts heads with other dinosaurs!

9. Paint the details of the "hard head."

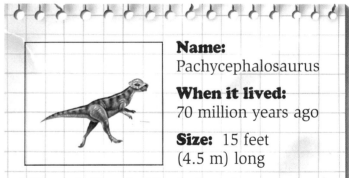

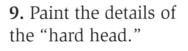

Name:
Pachycephalosaurus

When it lived:
70 million years ago

Size: 15 feet
(4.5 m) long

Where it lived: North America

Characteristics: Pachycephalosaurus was the largest member of a group of hard-headed dinosaurs. All of these dinosaurs had very thick skulls used for attacking and defending themselves from male rivals. Pachycephalosaurus walked with its back curved. It used its tail for balance.

A scary Stegosaurus

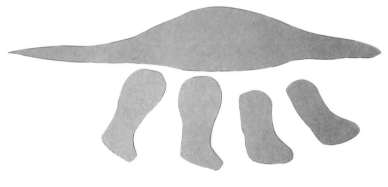

1. Draw the outline of Stegosaurus's main body and legs on posterboard, as shown. Cut the pieces out with scissors. Tape the legs to the body, two on each side.

2. Crumple newspaper into balls, and tape the balls to both sides of the posterboard.

You will need:
- tape
- Plaster of Paris roll
- containers of water
- scissors
- tempera paints
- posterboard
- newspaper
- a paintbrush

3. Be sure to tape balls of paper to the legs, too.

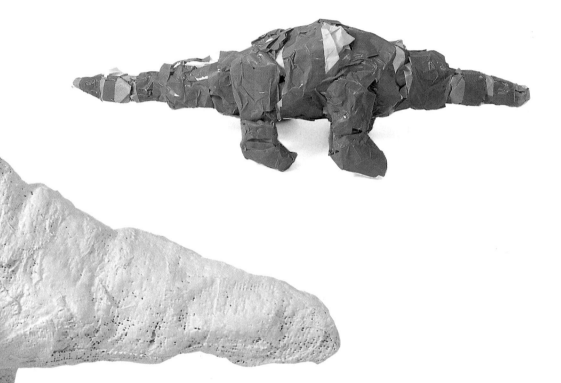

5. Then cover the entire dinosaur with the strips.

4. Cut short strips from a roll of Plaster of Paris. Place them in water for a few seconds.

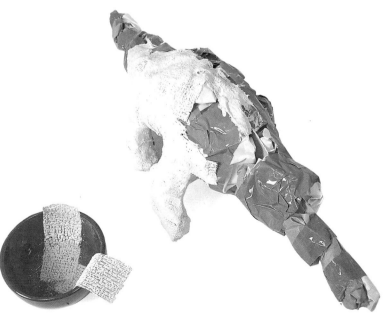

7. Cover the plates with strips of plaster, and let them dry.

6. On posterboard, draw some plates for the dinosaur's back, as shown. Cut them out with scissors. After making sure the the plaster on the dinosaur is dry, tape the plates to the dinosaur.

10. Twist some newspaper into spike shapes, and tape the spikes to the end of the dinosaur's tail. Paint them white. Finally, paint in details, such as the dinosaur's claws.

8. Paint the Stegosaurus light yellow. Let this color dry. Always wash your brush between colors.

9. Paint the plates and markings on the body with darker tones.

Name:
Stegosaurus

When it lived:
140 million years ago

Size: 30 feet
(9 m) long

Where it lived: North America

Characteristics: Stegosaurus was a medium-sized dinosaur that had large plates running down its back. These plates acted like solar panels to control the dinosaur's body temperature. The plates could absorb the sun's rays to provide warmth. The plates could also retain coolness in case the temperature of the air became too hot.

A roaring Parasaurolophus

1. Form the basic body shape of Parasaurolophus in modeling clay, as shown.

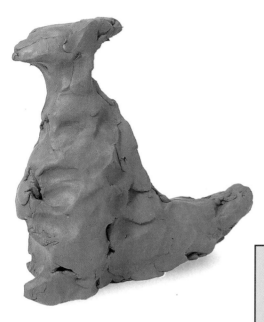

2. Shape the head and tail. Notice that the head has a long crest.

You will need:
- modeling clay
- palette knives
- tempera paints
- a paintbrush
- containers of water
- slip, which is made by mixing small chunks of clay with water until a paste forms

3. Use a palette knife to hollow out the eyes. Roll out two pieces of clay for the arms.

4. Attach the arms to the main body with slip.

5. Smooth the dinosaur with your fingers and a palette knife.

6. Shape the legs by removing clay from the model with a palette knife.

7. Smooth the head and neck with a palette knife. Also, use the palette knife to hollow out the mouth and nostrils.

8. Let the model dry for a day. Then paint the body with light yellow tempera paint. Next, paint brown markings on the dinosaur's back, as shown. Before changing colors, always let the previous color dry. Also, be sure to wash your paintbrush between colors.

9. Paint the nose and markings on the neck and chest orange.

10. Add some markings in red. Use white and brown for the eyes, and white for the nostrils and claws.

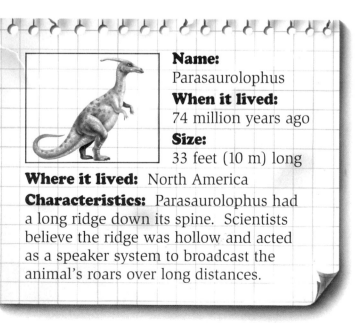

Name:
Parasaurolophus
When it lived:
74 million years ago
Size:
33 feet (10 m) long
Where it lived: North America
Characteristics: Parasaurolophus had a long ridge down its spine. Scientists believe the ridge was hollow and acted as a speaker system to broadcast the animal's roars over long distances.

A treacherous Triceratops

1. Draw outlines of the parts of Triceratops's body on posterboard, as shown. Cut the pieces out with scissors. Tape the legs to the body, two on each side.

You will need:
- a pencil
- scissors
- posterboard
- art paste
- tape
- newspaper
- containers of water
- a paintbrush
- tempera paints

3. Tape the head plate to the back of the head, as shown.

2. Crumple newspaper into balls, and tape the balls to the dinosaur, as shown. Remember to do both sides.

4. Prepare the art paste, and place strips of newspaper in it for a few seconds. Press the strips on the dinosaur, as shown. Let the model dry for a day.

6. Tape the horns to the head.

9. Finally, paint the horns, toes, and mouth white. Paint the tongue red, and the eyes black.

5. Twist some paper into horns, as shown.

7. Paint the main body of the dinosaur blue.

8. Let the blue color dry. Then paint green markings on the skin, as shown. Always wash your brush between colors.

Name:
Triceratops
When it lived:
Between 70 and 65 million years ago
Size: 36 feet (11 m) long
Where it lived: North America
Characteristics: Triceratops weighed as much as five rhinoceroses. The three horns on its head were used to fight other dinosaurs.

A daring Dimetrodon

You will need:
• papier-mâché
• a pencil
• tape
• newspaper
• posterboard
• a paintbrush
• tempera paints
• containers of water

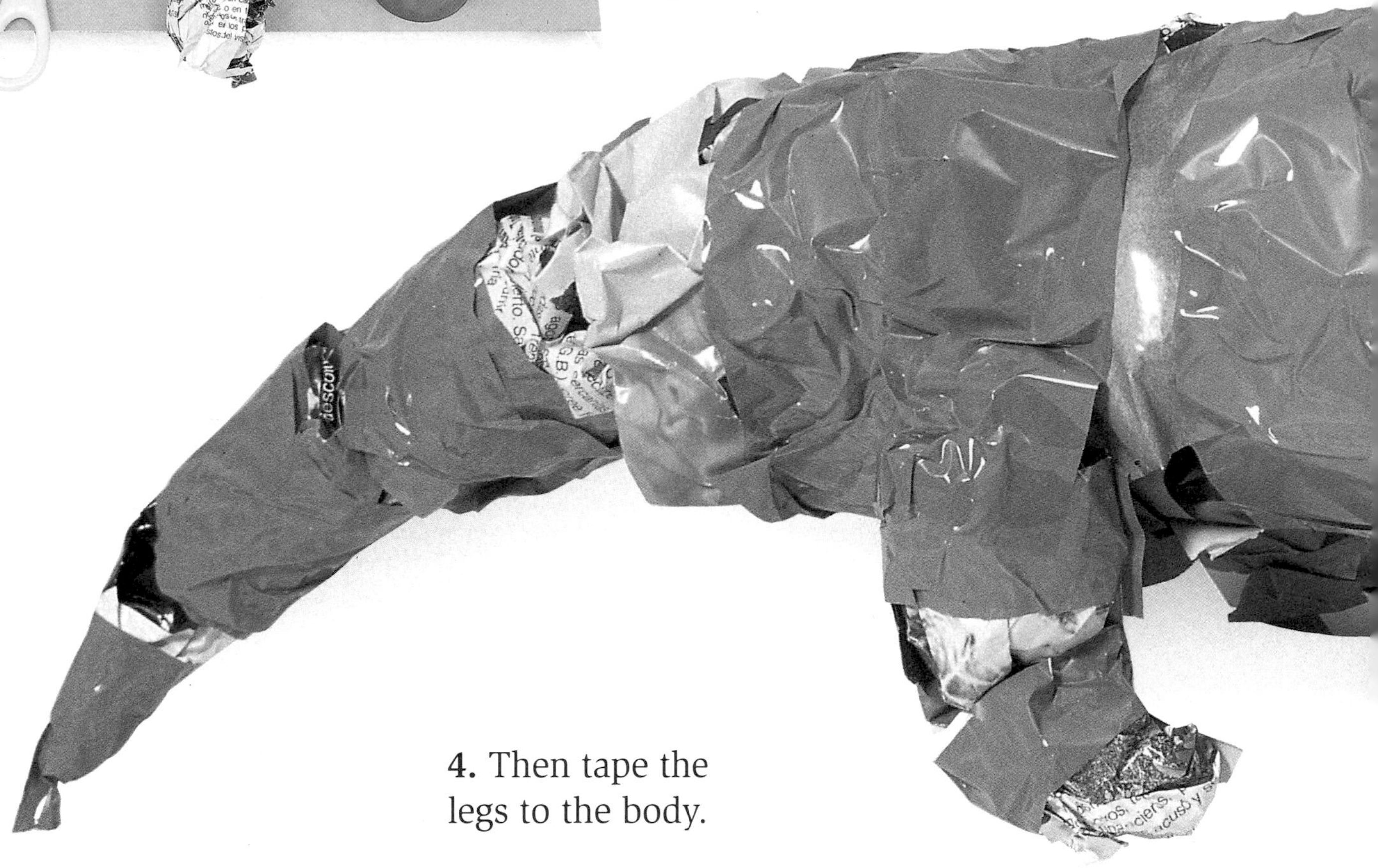

4. Then tape the legs to the body.

1. Draw an outline of Dimetrodon on posterboard as shown above. Cut the pieces out.

2. Crumple newspaper into balls, and tape the balls to both sides of the main part of the dinosaur's body.

3. Tape balls of newspaper to the legs.

5. Prepare the papier-mâché. Cover the entire dinosaur with the pulp. Press down firmly on the material with your fingers. Then let it dry.

6. Draw a crest, like the one shown above, on posterboard. Cut the piece out, and tape it to the main body. Then cover it with papier-mâché, and let it dry.

8. Wait for the paint to dry, and then paint details. For instance, add light green lines to the crest, and paint the eyes and teeth white.

7. Paint the main body green. Wash your brush, and paint the crest yellow.

Glossary

carnivore: an animal that eats meat as its primary source of food.

fossil: the remains of plant or animal life from long ago that is imbedded in rock.

herbivore: an animal that eats plants as its primary source of food.

media: a combination of styles, methods, and materials used by artists. Paint, crayons, chalk, Plaster of Paris, papier-mâché, sized paper, and modeling clay are media.

palette knife: a flat plastic or wooden tool used in sculpting and modeling.

papier-mâché: a modeling substance made from paper pulp. The term is French, and it means "chewed paper."

Plaster of Paris: a prepared mixture of sand, lime, and water that hardens and keeps a shape when it dries.

rivals: living beings that are in competition with one another.

slip: a substance used to bond pieces of clay together, made by mixing small chunks of clay with water until a paste forms.

tempera paints: paints that are mixed with water.

texture: the look or feel of a surface.

wire modeling tool: a tool used in modeling to hollow out or scoop clay. It is usually made of wood with a wire loop on each end.

Books and Videos for Further Reading

Animals At A Glance: Dinosaurs & Other Prehistoric Animals. Flügel (Gareth Stevens)

Clay Modeling for Everyone. Johnson (A. Schwartz and Co.)

Creating with Clay. Kaufmann (Van Nostrand)

The New Dinosaur Collection (series). (Gareth Stevens)

The New Dinosaur Library. Dixon (Gareth Stevens)

Worldwide Crafts (series). Deshpande and MacLeod-Brudenell (Gareth Stevens)

Dinosaur! The Fossil Rush: Tale of a Bone. (A & E Home Video)

The Infinite Voyage: The Great Dinosaur Hunt. (Vestron Video)

Index